I0121878

L.I.V.E.

Life Is Valuable Everyday

by

Linda Kay Jones

L.I.V.E. — Life Is Valuable Everyday

Linda Kay Jones

ISBN-10: 0-9977051-7-5
ISBN-13: 978-0-9977051-7-1

Library of Congress Control Number:2018904958

Copyright © 2018 Linda Kay Jones

All rights reserved.

For permissions contact: lkdavis0@gmail.com

Printed in the United States of America.

BELLA JOHNS ENTERPRISES
PUBLISHER

CONTENTS

ACKNOWLEDGEMENTS

I would like to thank Almighty God for giving me love for children, concern about the shedding of innocent blood and desire to speak out against gun violence. A special thanks to my mother, Della Austin, who encouraged me to move forward with my LIVE project. My children; David, Daniel, Della, Mary and niece Chantelle (who spent more time at my house than hers) who loved me in spite of the challenging times we endured, kept me encouraged and allowed me to use their children to get started. All of my beautiful grandchildren: Linda, Ashley, Justin, Daniel Jr., Jeremiah, David Jr., Dana, Azaria, Riley and niece Katrina, who put up with me taking numerous photos along with asking lots of questions. Thanks to Divine Faith World Christian Church, under the leadership of Apostle Kenneth Haywood, Co-Pastor Anita Haywood, the Drama Ministry team, my wonderful youth: Jason, Shajirrah, Jariel, Jamari, Zykerria, Macayla, Lavell, Nathanial, Ari, Sarah, Rebekah and Hannah. Thanks to Burnham Math and Science Academy principle Dr. Linda James Moore, who allowed her students to participate in LIVE workshops along with Dr. Billie Poe who brought us together. Finally, I would like to thank Jo McEntee from Writers Workshop who helped me get the LIVE book published.

INTRODUCTION

L.I.V.E. was birthed out of my anger from watching the news reports of innocent children being slaughtered on the streets of Chicago. In September of 2015, I gathered my grandchildren and shot a video called "put the guns down we want to grow up" and "a life is a terrible thing to waste". However, a lot of changes took place in my life that cause me to put the L.I.V.E. project on the back burner. After having fun with the children from Burnham Math and Science Academy in the intergenerational gardening and fitness programs in June 2016, Dr. Poe asked if I would volunteer to work with the children in the July 2016 summer program. I accepted the job, retrieved my L.I.V.E. project and began mentoring children on how to live a long life by avoid guns in conjunction with respecting others.

In the LIVE mentoring program, the youth learn about children who lost their lives from gun violence. They also have an opportunity to grieve their loss designing a poster in remembrance of the relative or friend who was killed by guns. The children interact with Chicago Police Department thru CAPS where they can ask questions, learn how to be safe at school, home and why it is important to avoid playing with guns. Additionally, they have a chance to express their selves through arts and crafts by designing necklaces, bracelets and T-Shirts. Finally, the children are videotaped saying what they want to be when they grow up and singing the LIVE song.

The children—ages six through nineteen—presented in this book are from the following programs: Burnham Math and Science Academy 2016 summer program and the fall afterschool program, Divine Faith World Christian Church 2016 drama ministry, Supernatural Flames of Fire Ministries June 2017 Conference.

L.I.V.E. gives youth an outlet to grieve the loss of a relative or friend due to gun violence, realize the value of life, learn to avoid gangs and hanging out with the wrong people. In addition to teaching youth the danger of playing with guns and importance of obtaining a good education. Finally, they learn to respect their selves, others, adults and those in authority.

KATRINA ALEXANDER

"When I grow up I want to be a special education teacher because I love children, especially those that have medical needs."

ABENA AMOAKOHENE

"When I grow up I want to be a movie star so I can be on TV because I have never been on TV. Living is good because you can do stuff. If you don't live, you can't do stuff you've never done or see something you've never seen."

ERASMUS AMOAKOHENE

"When I grow up, I want to be a policeman."

TOMICKA ANDERSON

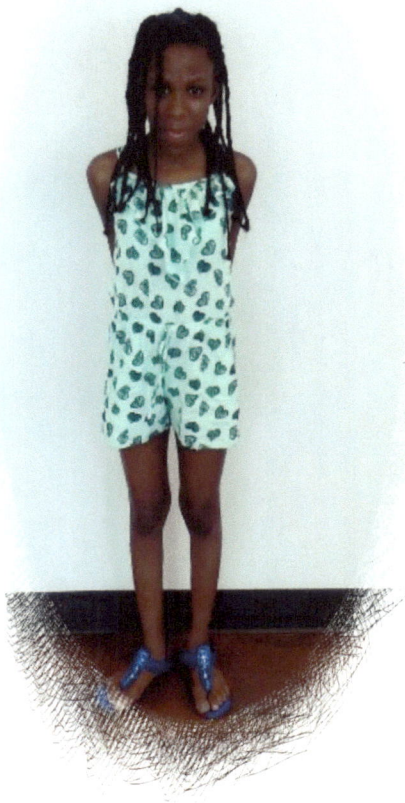

"When I grow up I want to be a pre-school teacher. Life is important because if you don't grow up to be what you want to be, you won't get a chance to do everything like everyone else."

KALIAYA BENSON

"When I grow up, I want to be a nurse so
I can help people feel better."

ASIA CARTER

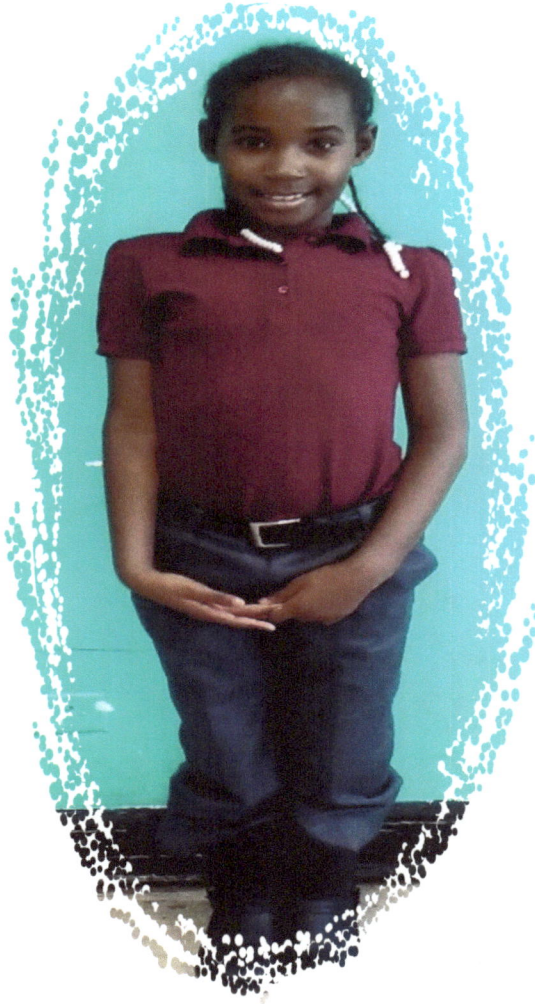

"When I grow up, I want to be a lawyer so I can give back to the community. It is important to live because if you don't live you won't be able to have your dream. When you grow up, you can do your dream and accomplish all of them. You can help other people, that's what Thor Soderberg did and that's what I want to do when I grow up because he was a kind person. He was a police officer and a good officer."

DANIEL FARRELL

"Life is very important every day because you only have one chance to do what you want in life. Whether it means being a tumbler, a game designer or anything else. So the reason that some people don't get to do what they want to do is because of gun violence. Guns are being used accidently, purposefully and using guns is just bad. So that means if we want everyone to live, we need to stop gun violence. STOP IT!"

ANTHONY FLOWERS

"When I grow up, I wan to be a policeman so I can help people stay calm and not be frightened."

TRISTAN FRAZIER

"When I grow up, I want to be a policeman so I can help people."

ARI HAYWOOD

"When I grow up, I want to be a Pediatrician."

NYLAH HUNT

"When I grow up, I want to be a firewoman so
I can help people be safe from fires."

JARIEL JOHNSON

"When I grow up, I want to be a teacher, or actor because I do a lot of acting."

SHAJIRRAH JOHNSON

"When I grow up, I want to be a sports manager
or doctor because I like helping people."

HANNAH JONES

"When I grow up, I want to be a soccer player because I like playing soccer."

REBEKAH JONES

"When I grow up, I want to be a
veterinarian because I love
taking care of animals."

SARAH JONES

"When I grow up, I want to be a lawyer so I can help people."

ARMON KELLY

"When I grow up, I want to be a NFL professional football player and help our community. It is important to live because if you don't live, you cannot learn stuff. It's also important because you take experience from life and give experience to life."

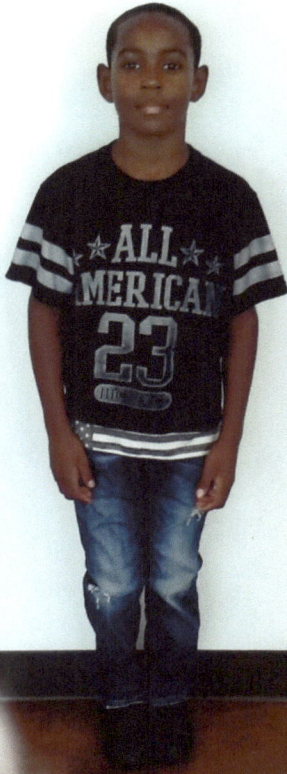

LINDA MONAE KING

"When I grow up, I want to be
a political science professor."

JAMES LINTON, JR.

"When I grow up, I want to be a police officer, so I can help people like Jesus did."

JAMARI LOGAN

"When I grow up, I want to
be a basketball player."

KYAN LOWE

"When I grow up, I want to be
a pet keeper."

JUSTICE MANU

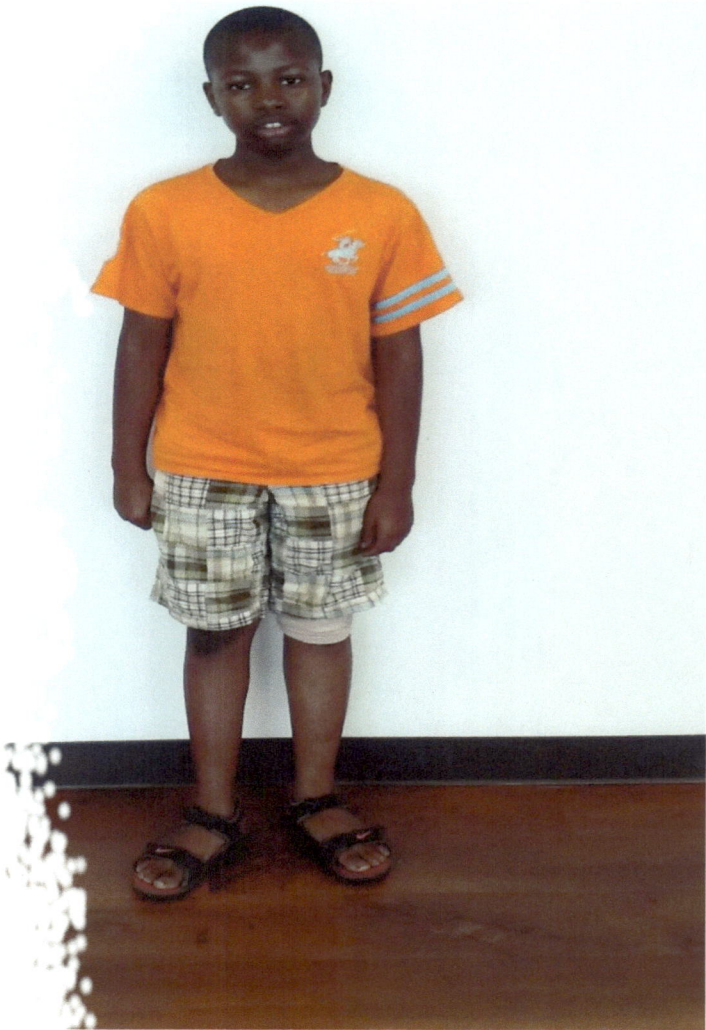

"When I grow up. I want to be a crossing guard. Life is important because everybody should have a future of what they want to be."

ALONTA PARKER

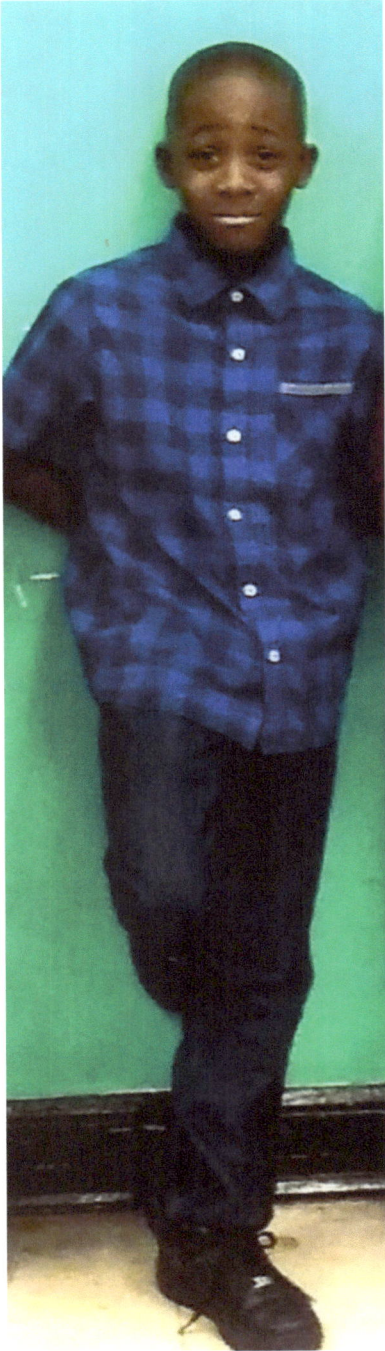

"When I grow up, I want to be a doctor so I can help people so they will not die."

JASON LAWRENCE HENRI PORTER

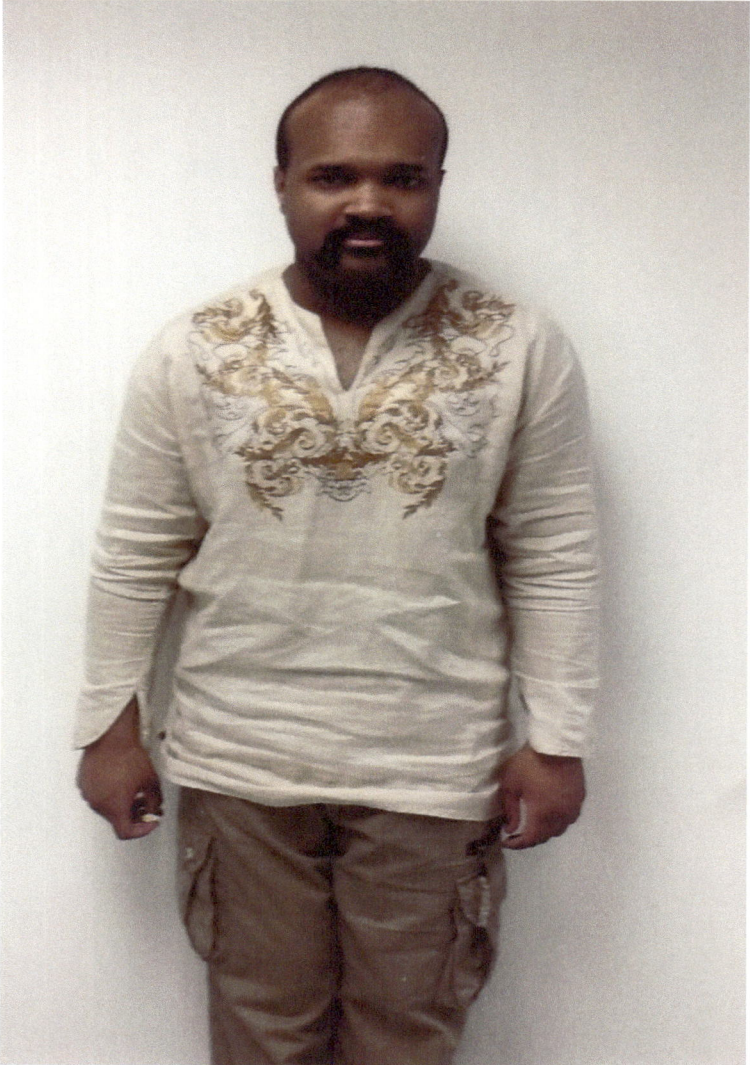

"When I grow up, I want to be a teacher because I like to help people."

JEREMIAH EMANUEL ROBERSON

"When I grow up, I want to be a
Graphic Designer."

NATHANIAL DEMETRIUS SIMON

"When I grow up, I want to be an artist."

ASHANTI TOLIVER

"When I grow up, I want to be a teacher so I can teach children what I have learned in grammar and they can be teachers when they grow up."

RILEY LOUIS WALSON, III

"When I grow up, I want to be a professional basketball player."

YARIAHNI WASHINGTON

"When I grow up I want to be an Olympian like Gabby Douglas. I think people should live because if they don't live, they won't get to do what they dream about."

LAVELL WILLIAMS

"When I grow up, I want to be a teacher because I like to teach."

MACAYLA WILLIAMS

"When I grow up, I want to be a
teacher so I can dress
professional."

MARISSA WILLIAMS

"When I grow up, I want to be a teacher because I love helping children learn. One day I will go to college and get a degree."

MESSIAH WILLIAMS

"When I grow up, I want to be a doctor so I can make people feel better."

Zykerri Wailliams

"When I grow up, I want to be a teacher or a policewoman so I can help people."

JAQUAN WILSON

"When I grow up, I want to be a police officer so I can protect people from danger."

ASHLEY AMARI WOLFE

"When I grow up, I want to
be a magazine writer."

AZARIA WOLFE

"When I grow up, I want to be a photographer or Paleontologist because I like taking pictures and discovering old things from back in time."

DANA WOLFE

"When I grow up, I want to an entrepreneur and cosmetologist because there should be more female entrepreneurs and I love doing hair as well as make-up."

DANIEL MATTHEW WOLFE, JR.

"When I grow up, I want to be a professional football player."

DAVID GARDNER WOLFE, JR.

"When I grow up I want to be a philanthropist so I can build a center that will make people smile, improve their confidence and be proud."

JUSTIN WOLFE

"When I grow up, I want to be a chef, because I love cooking."

www.ingramcontent.com/pod-product-compliance
Lightning Source LLC
Chambersburg PA
CBHW041226270326
41934CB00001B/14